The Beast of Revelation 13

The Beast of Revelation 13

**The Number of a Man: Six Threescore and Six?
OR
Six Threescore to the Power and Six? = Nine?**

Lee Dawkins

Exposition Press   *Smithtown, New York*

FIRST EDITION

© 1982 by W. Lee Dawkins

ISBN 0-682-49887-4

Printed in the United States of America

STORY: Of how the white man and the beast (Satan) are one and the same. Spoken of by Jesus and Matthew, Daniel, also Ezekiel and the prophets from Holy Scripture.

MORAL: What all white human beings should come to know and understand: who they are, what their purpose is in life, and what their destiny is. And most of all, why the white man is seen as the master race.

Contents

The Beast of Revelation 13

To God, time is like a thousand years and a thousand years is to God like the wink of an eye. To show that since it is such to God, then this is the last thousand years that Satan is to be unleashed; also that this is the last generation—the year 2000.

1

The Beginning

My story is based upon many years of study of the white flight throughout history. It is also based upon my living with them, sleeping with them, being married once to one, being in the military with them, dreams, prayer, and ten years of Bible study.

To start my search, for some reason, I was so confused over the man having the number of "Six hundred three score and six." So I said to myself, if I can figure out that number, something told me I could unlock the whole mystery of the races and why things are as they are. Why the white man seems to have everything and suffers less than any other race. Why he is a minority of all the races and yet can rule with an iron hand. And what really makes him tick! All races have something in common, but the white man is not the same—and all for a very good reason.

First, let me go back to the age of seven for a very important reason that I was later to find out: why me? It was early one summer morning in the city of Berkeley, California, where I was born. I'll never forget, as long as I live, what happened to me. It was about seven or eight o'clock in the morning. My mother had gone to the neighbor's for coffee, as she always did after my father left for work. School was out for the summer, and some friends and I were to go up to the Berkeley hills to play and pick plums. I left my house and went across the street to get my best friend and see if he was still going with me and the rest of the boys. His name is Roy Bayless. On the way, I had to cross Sixth Street, and the early morning traffic was typically bad. I crossed the street without any problem. I had to walk around the side of Roy's house because the front of his home was facing the opposite way from the street. As I walked alongside of his house, I was looking down, and to my amazement I saw a five-dollar bill, which must have blown there from somewhere. I picked it up and, boy, I was so excited I forgot to get Roy! I then turned, and the first thing I thought of was to go and show my mother what I had found. I had always been very alert, but from all the excitement, I forgot the street I had to cross. I was running as fast as I could. I ran out into the street without looking. At that very moment I heard a car's brakes squeal. I turned and looked—the car was right upon me. I knew I was dead, but the car went right over my path! In one split second, something with two huge hands filled with power took me by the shoulders and set me back where I had come from—back to the sidewalk. I turned to see who it was. There was no one. It was a clear, bright, Sunday morning, and as I looked up to see the face of who had those hands . . . what I saw I will never forget.

The day was made night, and I saw all the heavens. There standing among all the stars was a man clothed in a long white robe with gold around the neck, the bottom, and over his feet. Where the head was to have been there was no head but a face with a smile made out of the stars! The image of the face spoke to me and said, "Worry not. All was all right."

And then it was day again. The entire event was, to me, done all in a flash. The people in the car all thought I was dead, that they had run over me. They could not believe what had happened to me. I ran on when the street was clear. But I did not go to where my mother was. I went back to my house and just sat there for at least two hours. I was in total disbelief of what had happened. I would be unaware of this until two years later when something else happened. It wasn't until I was thirty years old that I was to find out what all this meant, and the reason why I now must write this book. So maybe, just maybe, a few whites can be saved before the end of time. And even if I can't make it, to save one is better than none of a race of people that I have admired all of my life—only because we are all of the same. All of one and one of all.

All of the following happened to me and are unexplainable to the normal human being. At the age of nine, I used sign language to explain to my older sister that I was dying because a large, candy jaw-breaker was lodged in my throat. At the age of fifteen and a half, while in Seoul, Korea, a two-and-a-half-ton truck turned over on me, but I escaped without a mark! Twice in a head-on car collision and not a mark. And once my right hand was pulled into a power machine. It was all cut up and almost completely off, yet it healed back to normal. At the age of thirty, I was divorced from a white woman in a white court, and all was taken from me through tricks and race hatred. I was left in New York without money, food, or shelter. All my personal belongings were stripped from me. I did nothing wrong. And afterwards I just sat and prayed, and more was given unto me than what was taken. Twice as much, without lifting a hand, in 1975, and it would secure me for the rest of my life.

I was without a home in Germany and, for over six months, without a penny, and yet I was cared for without saying a word until I returned to America in December 1975. I have had over five hundred white girlfriends from all over the world, and many more encounters. They and my wonderings have led me to an understanding of the whites.

I am telling you, the readers of this book, that I speak from the heart and with a very sound mind. I have the head of an IBM machine—do not forget what I write to you. I know that this book and my words will come down very hard on you and the white race. But history cannot be changed. So now through my poems, I will show you your destiny. And through my gift from. . . . Who knows but I?

I will unravel the mystery of The Beast to you that is written in Revelation 13:1 through Revelation 17, and I will work backward. To do this is to start at the end! For the first is the last, and the last is the first. I will open your eyes as to why you are white and I agree to you being the master race. But only because you are a dreamer. To understand me—for you it should be very easy—I will do it your way.

Also, in my book there is a question and answer to your role; why there is a difference between what you may have thought is, and was, but is not; and just why you are, as it may seem to be, the master race.

2

I Have a Dream

Now comes the third dream. We all have heard so many times from so many people and ministers about just who and what the Four Horsemen are that are spoken of in Revelation. I have in my second and third dreams been shown that I must write this. So pray that you will understand what I say unto the righteous and to them the meek of this generation!

I was shown that the Four Horsemen were that of one, the first, the white horseman with the white horse. The "bow" that this horseman had in his hand was deceit, which was that of the three remaining horsemen—of the colors red, black, and pale. The white horseman was of a race of people that would rise up in history to carry out the works of Satan. The other three horsemen and their works were all that of the first horseman, which was that of the first, the red—blood—which the horseman would cause with his booms, submarines, jets, helicopters, gunships, and so on.

Afterward, there would come the black horseman. The black rider, who was also part of the white horseman, would *starve* out all those not of the *white horseman* kind and make *death* to them *all,* because they were of the one God and not of the *many gods* that the white horseman really believed in! Because of this, the fourth horseman, the pale horseman, would try and finish off that third part of the people that did not obey their god. I say again to all those who have an ear—PRAY—that you understand, for I have been shown what to write to you! Not in doctrine, but with my writings you are being shown that this generation shall not pass. But, most important, pay close attention to the race that is in charge of the world, and what the

4

color of this race is. To understand your problems and my problems in these last days, you must understand the meaning of the horsemen, which is *them of one* and *them of a race of people!* Not that of a *horseman* or *men,* but that of a race of people.

Again, be very aware of myself as a beggar. The mark that is placed in your forehead is very important. The mark in your forehead is marking the color of your skin, and is not a true mark. So uncover the works of all four horsemen, and you, then, will have the prophecy of the Four Horsemen.

Remember what Martin Luther King, Jr., saw? Remember it was not of this world! So, I pray that you do not think that my dreams and writings shall all be shown to you before this generation ends. I am he of the (red) blood cell, my "gift" is that of the Spirit. . . .

First you must understand the wonders of God. A beast is that which will devil anything that gets in its path. The beast spoken of in Revelation is a people! A very certain kind of people, or being, which God had created and later came to scorn, scorn because of their inequities. Later on they became the workers of Satan. They were found to be unclean, the same as Satan!

I pray that you will understand what you read from here on. First, you must read the Book of Revelation. Start with Rev. 13:1, and read all the way through to chapter 17. When you have finished these chapters, to unravel the mystery you must look back at your history to the time of England, which was the start of the whore, the cause of the blood and the killing for a thousand years—a thousand years!

Pray that you will have understanding, for my words are true.

To teach you, we must uncover the meaning of the beast, the beast having seven heads and ten horns! Now, the beast is of seven diffrent lands or countries, and of the people of those lands.

The five that have fallen are: the first Babylon, Egypt, Assyria, Persia, and Rome. All these were empires. Afterward, the two remaining of the seven, were Alexander the Great, made up of

Greece, which is also the people of Britain, one and the same people!

The ten horns the beast had upon its head were those of its people, who were white, and dwelled in these ten lands: the British Empire, Russia, North America, Poland, Yugoslavia, Germany, Australia, France, Scandinavia, and Spain. These make up the "powerhouse" of Satan!

Then a beast came up with two heads, which are America and Russia, the Bear. They, too, are of the seventh head of Britain, a white race of people that split up and later became two beasts. The first would be Russia, and later would come America. Russia would fall in World War II, but would be later heralded by America, in what would prove to be America's downfall.

The slain beast, Russia, would and will become the strongest, like we've never seen before. Remember all the beasts are of the whites. The numbers are written in their heads, which are the color of the skin, or the color of the people that are concerned for the white race of white blood.

This is my white brother. Read, Daniel, the eleventh chapter and it will open your eyes. Be sure and read the entire chapter, verses 1 through 45, for this I show you not in doctrine . . . and, my man, there is no other race. No, not any like you that has done like so . . . nor shall there ever be another.

I pray that you understand. For my job is to be your toy—for your joy! Yes, I am the beggar, the weak, the meek, and I shall mourn for you when the game is over.

Oh, white man, if only it was just a fairy tale. Read for yourselves in Daniel 12. Read it all, for it is very important that you do. The whiteness is not of your color, but of the cleanliness of your soul!

Now I will give you the true meaning of the mystery of the whore! Foretold, and after I will cite for you your destruction. Do not forget that you have claimed throughout the years that you are the master race. Well, so be it!

Now, the whore is of the race of people who would lay in bed with all her love, lust, greed, and all inequities. To climb in bed with any of the people and do what she wanted to do—this is the same as what the whites have been doing and are doing: any and all things that would displease the one God!

If you will recall, a man called Jesus was offered the same things while he wandered in the wilderness for so many days. What other race have you ever seen or heard of to do this? Remember, five have fallen, then six and seven, but all were of the same, and white!

No one to this day has carried out the powers of Satan more than you, the whites. No others have fought against the might of God as you have done. To go hungry, be poor, and not make wars and rumors of war—does this get blamed on me, also, the way you are?

It has been stressed all through history to all believers to be most aware of the false prophets. They are very smart and wise. All you have taught me, and your own, is false doctrine. Would a true God be so cruel and make me suffer all these years? In the end, would He give you all the goodies, as now? All because you are white?

In this case, what you are telling me is there is no wrong? Do you really think I believe that? If that was the case, there would be no need for Him to come back and save the world. For Almighty God knew that the white man was unclean, that he would make a sword that would kill himself. The white man, you, have laid the way to self-destruction. Do you not complain more and more each day about your H-bombs? What all the H-bombs could do if you, your white brothers, and the Russians decide to have a go at it. What is this? Two brothers fighting one another. You have killed so many black brothers that you are confused now and you must kill your own! Read Revelation, chapter 12, verses 1 through 17.

All men who do as the white man has done, has in fact climbed into bed with the whore. The mystery of the bed is all the lands that the white man and his followers possess. His wonders are what you see, but he can keep them but for a little time: the travels, the car, another man's heart, kidney, or eyes by transplant. Be wise. For all the white man has learned over the past two thousand years is that which he has killed for and taken from other men in the far-off lands that were not his.

Yet, from all of this you are not happy. You have it all now, yet you grow weary. So be wise. You have the guns, the bombs. I am letting you know just how close you are to revelation of the opening of the seventh seal, and to that which was told by Matthew in chapters 24 and 25.

The trigger is Iran, which is Persia. That would join the Bear! Russia and all its bands would come out of the north like a whirlwind upon Israel in the last days. Now, tell me, do you think it will be five hundred years more before that takes place?

I say to you, the world has moved very fast and all the time you have been asleep. It is not your move, white man, but that of the very elect, the one God that you have so long denied.

But how, oh, white man, could you be the master race and so superior, yet so dumb?

To fool, not me, but you, I will flash before your very own eyes your tricks and your works. But remember, God has said you will be judged by your works.

3

Behold! I Am the Trumpet Player!

I have a blessing upon me! Have you an ear? Then come! Wo-o-o-o-o-o-o-o-o-o-o! It is almost time for the running of the seventh! The final race. So, come quickly and see!

We have great entries! War! Seen like never before, and the odds are a hundred-to-one in favor.

Behold, our second note! That we take great pride! He is called earthquake in many places. Have you not noticed him lately on the world news?

Like a thief in the dark, he comes without warning. For me, I am the trumpet player! The seventh and the last of its kind. I have shined and polished my "horn" for the last and final race.

We have a new horse, and its rider is a well-known jockey, by the name of Jesus! Behold, have you not heard of him? As for me, all you gamblers, I am called Gabriel, the soul horn player.

I shall blow for you like never before. Even so, the whole world may hear, but we must hurry. There are but five clicks before the start of the handicap—the seventh race.

Be wise and place your bets. The horse you see now is called Time, and some consider him of little value. But, be aware, for he may seem useless, but he is the day and night watchman.

Come! See the third; it is of what was, and is to come. The horse is Death.

The three martinis, he so enjoyed each day, was looked down upon, and all his free trips around the world—free of charge! Yes, free of charge because of the gift of your taxes that he has taken, which he did not share with you.

Behold! Much has been overlooked for our next eternity!

The horse and the rider with the stamp for your forehead has been overlooked. Some say it is your Social Security number, and he that wears it comes in under what is called the Justice Department. Have you not heard of such a horseman to come?

Come quickly, for I have but little time to prepare for the furlong, for the track is full of unbelievers. Yet, you come to make a wager that may cost you your life. The horses are approaching the starting gate. May God be with you. Come. Come and see!

The last collector is called the Internal Revenue Service, and its rider is of great means, for the IRS's true meaning is *I*llegal *R*epresentation of *S*ociety!

Now the horses and riders are in the gates. They're off and running. In the start, it's Power and Confusion, neck and neck. Following by a length is Chaos Worldwide. In fourth place is Unrest, ridden by Egypt, Israel, Lebanon, Ethiopia, India, Vietnam, China, South Africa, Rhodesia, Cuba, Angola, Spain, America, Russia, Iran, Cambodia, and the Warsaw Pact.

In fifth place, by a half-length, it's Oil, and the rider is Amoco-Shell-Mobil-Standard-Texaco-Exxon. This rider is the swordsman. He has a number of records for fixing prices, over-charging, price-fixing, and income-tax evasion.

Five lengths away and ridden by a jockey named Pleasure Seeker is the horse named Great Wealth and Power. He desires to increase his pay as much as fifty percent and hold all others to a mere seven percent. This horse is a threat to the outcome of this race, which is only a furlong. And coming around the clubhouse turn is Last Place.

Two of the horses are neck and neck, Japan and Germany, and moving up very fast. These two horses and their riders are twins. Their names are Greed and Self-interest. They will surely try for a last-minute rally.

Entering into the stretch is Confusion. Second, The Glory Horse, and the jockey, Jesus! This horse is like none other, and the strength is in his master, the first and the last.

Wo-o! I say, Wo-o-o-o! I am the trumpet soul player. I have blown my horn, for there is but one winner, and no finish is to be a photo finish!

Behold, I say! The stakes are high. Yet you seem to worry not. Shall it be you are a fool? For in this there are no racketeers, gangsters, or Mafia. The race is held by the power of the trumpeteer. For I am back to complete my job, and it was to blow the last tune—for the coming of the end!

There is only one winner, the jockey called Alpha and Omega!

I am Gabriel, the soul trumpet player! The tune I play is called "Salvation," not "Name That Tune."

I see sweat upon your foreheads. Could it be for fear you have lost your wager? And with your ear you heard not of what was the entry? Surely it was foretold before the beginning of the race!

"Like hell!" you say. I can assure you, it is like hell. Now I must go, for the end is near. Praise be to God.

W-o-o-o. And the last wo-o-o!

4

I Have a Dream

This is the first dream that I had, and I was shown how to unveil the meaning of the dream. Yet there is none that can undo the dreams as myself. Also, I was shown that many would look down upon me and others would wonder. Also, that many shall hate me. Some will be amazed by the truths of the writings, as will be the hearts of all those that are in doubt. It shall be proven to them so that they may also pray that they may understand as I have. Many fools will pray, speak wonders, show to make believe they received what they had prayed for, even though it was not! In this case many will fail to believe. Because it is really the heart of each person that truly shall be shown who is the beast spoken of in Revelation: chapters 13 to 17.

You can be very sure a fool will believe just about anything that he or she is taught, or told in these last days. So I say to each and everyone, big, small, rich, poor, preacher man, pope, beggar or thief: Be aware of all beggars! They are the rich! Also, to all those who yet have an ear, let them hear what the Spirit says unto the churches and not always just to those who sit in the churches; nor those that speak to others in the churches.

Take a parable that was given to me: If a world leader truly believed in the one God, would he or she then have to be born again? Shall they all be born again after they have been caught cheating those who first put them there. Has it already been said that they all were blessed by just being an American? Then is it what I say it is, Church versus Government? For truly I know! And truly I shall show you! Most important, not in doctrine, but as my book continues this is how I will uncover the meaning of the first dream.

12

> But at the very end of time, man's tongue has made
> him go blind *and not see!*
> For that time is near to the end of self-destruction!

Following is the dream, and afterward the interpretation of
self-destruction, self-induced, for self-born-again Christians. . . .

Praise the Lord that each and *everyone* understand what
I say unto all and unto *all* that read the following dream. This
is not that of a poet. Nor is it meant to be understood as poetry.
For a wise man or woman will surely not be misled into false
doctrine from what I have been shown to write.

Read the following for nothing can or shall be changed!

THE ROLE!

Why, oh, white man! In all your lands you couldn't withstand
the grace of that man that gave you the chance. That you were
once part of the same as me for with all your ways and hate'n,
now come tell me you are not that of Satan!

Behold and understand—my main white man! Take the
parable of your very own tongue, Matthew, chapter 15, verses 1
through 26: For your tongue is that of prophecy. There is no
other race of such or ever will be, for there is no more time for
me to do it!

If you are of the "red-headed blue-eyed" Christ from days of old,
then why did he leave you in charge to cause all of this? And not
for me to do it? Why do you not do his will—but your will? For if
you, my white man, are all right, then why is He, the very elect,
coming back? For me to believe in your joke, I've become a dope.
And truly I've missed the boat! White man! Why have you not
held the sick, comforted the meek, stopped the weeping, rested
my bones, put your weapons into plows? Most of all, why have you
not brought all the children unto you? Where is the relief of my
pain? Am I insane? For, my white brother, you have taken my
mother and sold her to another, so now you have become gods,
and by what means?

What has happened to Satan? God does not kill, steal, lie, and seven others. What can you say to me? For now you have eleven commandments! And at last you have taken to the television airwaves to preach to the world that you found God! Did it take you two thousand years to do just that? I say beware of the preacher man! He has killed the sheep. Look at the clothes he wears—all are made of lamb's wool to cover the inequities that he does to the end.

As for you, white man, has it crossed your mind—ever—that there just may be far too many gods? Would a god predict his own destruction at the end, as you so have done? Tell me, would you burn your own selves forever and ever? Oh, yes! I can see it now. And tell me your hair would then become like that of lamb's wool, and your feet the color of burned brass or copper.

Revelation, verse 1 through 20.

Read Malachi, chapter 3, verses 1 through 18. Or more, shall you judge me for my rights or you as white? Shall I kneel and pray for a better day? And while my eyes are closed, will you again take my land away? But why should I lay and pray, if you are the god for today? To let you say, Now let's pray.

Matthew, chapter 24, verses 1 through 51. For my body is not my soul, or of your kind. I shall not dine or drink of your wine. Because in the midst of all this, all the land is "scorned"! And out of this, the "Beast of Revelation" is born?

How shall I say it? Oh, white man! That it is odd? To find you are no god. Behold! And understand the mystery of the Tares!

Matthew, chapter 13 verses 1 through 23. For what all you have told me, and yet is that! It is all right starving the third world or all those that are not white! It's okay to be gay, commit abortions, to fill all your jails with the poor, and your law is the only law—which is not that of God's law. If you are so sure of yourselves on this, claiming to be the master race, then as gods, why? Do we see you make atomic bombs? more diseases, like cancer, heart problems, leukemia? More suicides? And many hidden facts of your experiments to clone and make test-tube babies? At the same time to make a baby, you turn around and kill a baby that is made from man? Hitler of Germany once did the same! And for all these things, I shall pray for you.

Now to unveil to you the Tares. The mystery of the Tares! In the wheat that was spoiling, the whole field, the wheat that was gathered, were those people that loved the one God and lived according to His will and Commandments. The burning of the Tared wheat of the field was done by that people—YOU—the white man, because you had corrupted the whole field, which is the world. It was the field of life, so it had to be burned. The fire is the pit of Hell. Pray that you understand. To you I speak straight as an arrow, cold as the northern ice. It is deadlier than the A-bomb.

The following are the most important clues to guide you, for very few of you will be saved. My message is this:

Which of you will be that very few? The death of you is not the H-bomb, but the coming of the one God. And to think that it is that far off! Don't be a fool. The clock started clicking the day you killed your Savior—two thousand years ago—not now!

Come, I will show you and pray that you are wise and understand what I write to you. For I am humble to the truth and the heart to the righteous and deadly to the Beast. So now ask yourselves as the master race: Why is it whites hunger not, but the rest of the world does so? Is it because you are white? Because you're white you may sleep tonight? But again you must kill at the break of light.

Why must you always be right as white and others wrong? Do the submarines and H-bombs make you strong? Why must you live in clean, white clothing and be waited upon, as head of the throne. Because you're white? Or by the power of might? Why is it in all your countries, you weep no longer?

Why is it you must have all the gold, silver, oil, and cattle? Because you are white? There is nothing that matters, so I am a fool, you say, because I pray! And you fear the love that was given to you from all those whose land you took away. Tell me, why is it, O white man, to you your color is so sweet? Your hair so neat? If I am not white, I must bow down to your feet? If any is left, then can I eat?

5

Why Am I Led to Believe?

Truly I give you the answer to your flight, as being a white. Why was Moses born and accepted as a son of the pharaoh? Answer: Because he was not that of a white, but of another, that of a black, as an Egyptian. To be white in that land would have caused corruption. If a white man, an outsider of a different race, had been made to rule over Egypt and its people . . . if Moses was white, then how could he have been taken in unnoticed by the pharaoh's courts? (Read: Leviticus, chapter 13, verses 1 through 59.)

Why in the houses of the Lord is it not spoken of Moses marrying an Ethiopian—she was black. So was Sheba! Sheba was married to Solomon! (Read: Numbers, chapter 12, verses 1 through 11.)

Very important! Where did Noah's sons depart to? (Read: Genesis, chapter 10, verses 1 through 10.) For all the lands of Egypt were of Africa, and the Middle East was of the black race.

Why is it the Jews are scorned the same as the blacks? Because they, my brother, are one and the same. And why did God say that he would slay all those who say they are Jews, but are not? There are many different colors today in the Land of Israel that claim to be the true Jews. But there is a clause: blacks have been scorned and killed more so than the Jews, and also are in every—every—land as slaves, and are wanting to go back to their homelands. Even more so, tens of millions more blacks are killed than that of the white-man Jew. For America only helps Israel today because she is seen to be of the white race. If today Israel were to be black, do you think African whites and America would give her so much arms? No way, my man. If history has not shown it, the Germans have in World War II. Remember the hate the German has for the Jew, and South Africa is made up of the Jew's very enemy—the German. Why?

To conclude this of the beast: the white man's tongue has condemned the whole world. And all his miracles are the same as that of Satan, as spoken of in Daniel, St. Luke, Revelation, and St. Matthew. My brother and the world as it is now, the New Testament is that of which was and is and will be—for only two thousand years. All has been fulfilled, but one thing. Take it or leave it from me. But just could it be! I mean, just could it be that we're living in those last one hundred years?

For now I lay me down to sleep, I pray my soul for God to keep!

> End! O little town of Bethlehem,
>   Why did the white man not see the light.
>   Above the deep and dreamless sleep,
>   For him shall none WEEP!

6

I Have a Dream

First I will try and show the people and the world just what is in store for all of us as of this decade and the last few decades to come. I advise each and all to try and understand completely the way I reveal to you the meaning of that very important chapter of the Revelation, chapter 13. For giving a man one minute of my time, I was then shown all these things that were to come and end all things as we now see them. For what I say, I know. I will open your eyes, but not most of your hearts. For all those who have an ear, then read as follows: What wise man or woman will get my message? Because without a doubt, my words will hurt, slander, and confuse even those who already know this book is and will be a hard pill to swallow.

Now here is the second dream. There was the dragon and the beast, and both had swords on the tips of their tongues. The dragon used his hand to confuse part of the world with his pen, which was his tongue. That, I will show, is the American news media. Then there was the beast, with a tongue the same as the dragon's, and in his hand was a hammer and a sickle. But the beast took the other part of the world. First it cut down all those not in its favor with the use of his sickle, and the rest he hammered into submission.

The sickle of the beast was supposed to represent equal measures for all. Then, came the hammer, which was that of might and the use of power. You must always remember, I have stated throughout my book that the beast and dragon are really the same, and that both are of the northern parts. But be not confused, because these two are identical twins from the same family—white!

Take a parable of my second dream:

> For because of all the world's disbelief in God in these last days,
> Man's eyes have made him see and believe in what man says.

I will show each and everyone just why it is that we people of today are in such a mess and cannot get out of it. Now, if any man or woman cannot understand these writings, they are surely lost.

For now God has laid a sleep upon the world, before he is to come back as he had once promised the world he would. Now, why is it that nothing really seems to matter anymore, considering all the wrong things that are going on these days in the world, and that no one really seems to care either? Nor will they even try to lift or give a hand to change anything. Yes, it seems as though they are, but if you all will look at the very fine print, it is really not true that man wants to change anything unless it is for his or her own benefit. The reason is this, for I have been shown that God, not Satan, has moved the clock of life forward upon the whole world. Now, some will claim to have seen this as so, and others will just stagger on until the very end.

This is the fault of governments, the preacher man, the races and, most of all, you, the individual. Why do you think man has come so far in less than one hundred years with so many wonders and lustrous things? But in two thousand years he was left idling around the world not knowing very much. Also, because of all the wonders we now see around us made by man, it seems that man has made himself his own god. Nowadays, everything man does for the eyes is for pleasure, and it has made you and many others forget just what is really going on around yourselves. So I write this quote! The faster you accept all these things of man, then the faster it is that all our days are being shortened. Nowadays, it seems that the goodies are coming to everyone so quick and so much that lust has condemned the world in such a way that very few have stopped to see just what is going on around us all.

My words within ten years, I say, will not only show you,

but astound you! And you shall think and wonder just how I knew these things. For I am no god, nor do I claim to be. Now, because of what I have been shown, let's say I am a messenger. I have become afraid of what was shown before my very own eyes. People today think that they have it so bad. Well, we all haven't seen anything yet. We haven't seen what is to come. We haven't really looked at things, with nothing left out. Just what is it that we all have done to make this world a better place? A certain race of people did nothing but hide, cover up, betray, confuse, and consume to please themselves, at the same time thanking Jesus for all that they have taken with a gun; the race with the injustice, saying that GOD blessed them. In my teachings, I will prove all those wrong that claim fame and blessings.

To all those who have nothing, do not feel like a fool, for what you see ahead is nothing but problems, and more problems to come like never before. The race of people from the beast of Revelation, chapter 13, can surely be proven of who is who! All the sorrow and pain we see today are caused by that certain race of people. This I will show before your very own eyes. This is what I was shown through dreams, and I, as Daniel, was made to write this book in the fashion that I now write it. All of my writings will be borne out, not in another generation, but *this* generation. For after this generation, there is no more. With my gift I claim, as the writer of this book, to be greater than ERA, greater than your family doctor, more wise than all the scientists, more bold than the pope or preacher man.

If you think God has blessed you and I with all these problems, I say think again! For what you don't want to hear, read this book and I will show the world its own heart. I will come into your living rooms and your offices, your bedrooms, your churches, your colleges, and show that in this time and age, you are not blessed, though it may seem so. Nor are you, me, or anyone else, save as many who have so claimed to be. I hope that all readers don't feel left out because of what I write. But for all and all it shall be shown in fine print just why things are the way they are for a few and not for the many.

How fast you see people come to the rescue for lust, but

will you do the same after reading my writings? For all I write is to show you what Martin Luther King, Jr. tried to show you and the world. The road the world is traveling down is not, I repeat, is not the way to those gates. The gate you seek is that of self-distraction. If I seem like a fool to each and all, then I pray that you understand what it is that was put into a fool's head in order to write this book. I am a gambler and I say a hundred to one that most will not make it to the door or the gates. Place your bets on my words, the money will be your hearts and soul. My bet is what I have in cash, the cash of a blessing. It was given to me by a beggar man. I stopped to give him or her a dime one day. In return that beggar gave me a rock. And the beggar said to me, "Take this rock and throw it into a lake. If there are any fish in the lake, don't eat any, because the lake that you threw the rock into, is that lake made of water, no! But of fire! And here we eat no more fish or bread." The beggar then said, "Now for the dime that you gave to me was from my heart." Because that very dime was from his heart also. Because of that dime I gave to him without question, he then said in return, "I give you this last chance to show the entire world that this beggar made that dime and the rock also!" He then went on to say, "I shall claim all that [I] write in a book within these last one hundred years of the twentieth century, and that what I write shall not pass a hundred years."

So here I go. Let's all go back to when England first sent her misfits to America, or when Columbus first came to the shores of America. Columbus met the Indians, which shows someone was here before he came. Columbus then pretended to be a friend. We are told he then took Pocahontas to England to meet the queen. This proves God had already blessed America before the white man came. Later the armies came in the name of the queen, saying that they all came to enlighten those poor lost souls, the Indians. At that time the Indian was pure, clean, no diseases, no rapes, no guns, or whatever. Afterward, you know the rest. Now just who do you think was really blessed? Was it before the coming of Columbus, or after?

Now the Indians, they saw all the evil, cruelty, the disease, murder, and they wanted no part of it, for their people were already blessed. Then the white man started to kill, rape, and put these people into slavery. You all have heard that old saying, "A good Indian is a dead Indian!" Well, it's been that way ever since. The Indian, the nigger, the Jew, the Mexican, the Chinese— all those not of a certain kind were all called savage and ungodly.

We must also remember that at that time England sent all of her misfits, murderers, thieves, and whores to America. You name it. Now, *is this a blessing of God?* Don't be stupid!

But once you had claimed this land called America, God saw a little forgiveness in a few hearts for some of the whites. That started out well and good for all the people of this land we call America. So to check out the people known as our forefathers, it all started with the Constitution, which was the greatest document that was ever to be written, only if lived up to. But it has not been lived up to. For as we see it, America has never tried to live up to the Ten Commandments or the United States Constitution. If you all will just compare the two, it seems like a very big joke to all races but the white race.

This being the order of the society in charge, we have all been put under the feet of the beast and the dragon, which is and was quoted throughout the last testament of the Book Of Revelation. Now, if there is really anyone in the world who has not learned the truth of who the dragon is, I have been shown without a doubt that it is America, and the beast is Russia and all its allies. If each and everyone will do as I—think! Now, who in the world could stand up to or would dare try or even think they could beat or overthrow either of the two above lands that I've just described?

We all have heard many times that there is nothing wrong with a "little white lie." Well, I've been shown that those little white lies being told all over the world will cause the total destruction of the whole world in not too long a time. Because now we see that there is nothing worse than all those little white lies. The outcome of the struggle between these two empires will surely prove that they are the dragon and the beast. Remember

Hitler and all those wars for a thousand years past. Now, has not the Lord himself put in plain details that Satan would be unchained for a second and final thousand years after the crucifixion of Christ? Well, like I've stated and will state throughout my book, I advise you to be aware of the beggar, as I myself am. For I have a dream, and it won't be long—to belong.

7

Israel Foretells the End

Enclosed is a picture of what spoke to me and led me to write this book to the entire world. I drew the picture on canvas. It is exactly what I saw. I used my Polaroid camera to take a snapshot of my drawing. The photo shown is better than I had imagined it would be. This picture is what I saw in broad daylight. Now, for all those who cannot see in the picture what I see and what I saw, let me say this, just pray that you understand what the Spirit says unto the churches. This book is not science fiction, but you have the right to think it is. But I say this to all those in doubt, watch for what my book has tried to teach you before the last days, before the year two thousand in this decade, this generation! This is a picture of the Heavens around eight or eight-thirty A.M. on a very clear California summer day.

This statement is made with a very sound mind and with a very humble soul, by me, Webster L. Dawkins, son of Baby L. Dawkins, grandson of Wallace Dawkins.

Now, the larger part of the people in this world do not seem to really understand just why it is that the Arabs are so high-strung over Israel being a nation—with those people now living there in Israel. I say this to make you all understand just why this is so.

First, God was very angry with the Jews. The Greeks, who were white, started it all. Later would come the English, the Europeans, the Romans, and the Spanish. All these were of the white race. Over the centuries, the Jews became lighter and lighter in color. Because of this, the white men introduced the color differences within that area. Then as now, the whites claim that the Jews were of the white race. But be not misled anymore by who is really who! Before the invasion of the Holy Land by the white armies, there were no whites in Israel. Now, this is the very reason why the Arabs are so angry with the rest of the world today. They, the Arabs, have and were forced out of their land by the Americans, Russians, English, and the Germans, all for greed and a claim to fame. I say: Pray that you understand what I show you! For all the trouble that you now see in the Middle East was foretold by God. This is right on schedule with the fulfillment of God's plan.

Let's face it, the most important thing in life to the Arabs is and always has been their religion. They, the Arabs, will die for just that cause, above all else. Another very important thing for the Arabs is color. Color meant nothing in those days to them, because they were all of the same race and color until the whites inflicted this upon them.

Take a parable: An eagle does not kill a hawk, because a hawk is not an eagle, and the hawk can fly the same as the eagle. Nor does the eagle look at the color of the hawk, because what angers the eagle is that the hawk is in the area the eagle had before the hawk arrived. The eagle wants only what is rightfully his.

So shall it be for the true Jew. His land was given by God, not by man. Each of the following men has taken an eighth of my body and spirit: John F. Kennedy, Martin L. King, Jr., Egypt's Sadat, Tutankhamen, my baby brother, and most of all, my grandfather. My faith, because of such as these, is great—through Almighty God. Amen!

8

Repent! The Prophecy Nears

Now there is a final outcome to my prophecy. And that is, look around you at what television and the news media are telling you, me, and everyone else, and that is that you may do—anything—or whatever you feel like doing, no matter what the outcome.

Today we see sex as the top priority of and above everything else, before the feeding of millions of starving people all around the world except for the white society. This means something is very wrong in the world somewhere. That beast, spoken of by Daniel and Revelation's chapter 13, is very clear. Only a stupid fool and a beast will overlook the outcome. Just why are people today trying so hard to make excuses for why the Bible and prophecy have become so misleading? Well, I say this is not as you may think, because it is your very selves that are misleading because of your greed and inequities. Everyone in his or her heart knows for a fact that which is right and that which is wrong! And to prove my point to you and any other, read the King James version of Daniel, Matthew, St. Luke, and Genesis, and feel free to comply with those teachings. Then it is no wonder we are all having it so bad. Now, if in my closing chapters my words offend you, they are meant to do just that! Because you have angered the one God! And myself because of the very fact you have caused each and all to stand judgment before God, because you have misled many with your false doctrine, your tricks in sorcery, your magic and your evil corruption. Now this is and was foretold two thousand years ago. And the way things are today, I challenge you or anyone to a duel. And that is: my gift will prove that I speak with faith and what I have been shown, and that in no way will you or I be given, not even in two hundred more years on this earth, to anymore prove the one God wrong, or ever again be able to bring such a disgrace in his eyes, like what we all see happening. Do you recall the musical song done by the well-known Beatles, called "I am Taking the Easy Way Out?" Well, that was for them because they were not God's. But there is no easy way out when you face the real and one and only God! And brothers, that time is not very far off. To show you what I say and write to you, suppose you were all sitting at a dinner table in the kitchen and saw and smelled the food that you were about to eat. Then the same is for my prophecy—you have been sitting there already, aware and yet unaware of the meal that is being prepared for you. But out of all, mainly you, the beast of Revelations, the man with the number six, three times three and six. For my wickedness of writing to you is only to show you the gift of how I interpret to you that you may understand what I say to all those who have an ear, for there is but one item left on the agenda! Now who, or which of you do see and understand the meaning of my words? For all those that do, pray to God and not to me of what you have been shown not in doctrine. For without prayer, Satan cannot be beaten. Now, do you think otherwise? I say to you, Damn you! Because it will surely come to pass that you and many others will be damned. Praise the Saints. And remember: Never read a verse in Bible prophecy if you do not read the whole chapter. Now, in that way will you come to understand and see? That everything of God's word is right on time. Nothing has altered or changed since the showing and telling to Daniel of what was to come for you and me and what was to happen in order that only the truthful would understand before the very end.

Why is it that so very few do not see the sword and sickle of the news media and television and what they are really doing to the world as we once knew it? I know, but why not you? All for a very good reason. They are both of a teacher with his own classroom and his own private school. He may pass on the teaching of Gog and Magog, the Antichrist. Included are the soap operas daily shown, the sex orientation such as seen on Mike Douglas, Phil Donahue, "Good Morning America," Cable TV, where the X-rated sex is being shown for a price, "Three's Company," and many others. And to top it all are the countless murder shows like "Vegas," "Rockford Files," "Dukes of Hazzard," "Quincy," and others. They teach theft, rape, murder, sex, adultery, hate, greed, corruption, misunderstanding of society, false doctrine, and manipulation of brother and sister against one another. For all is a matter of brainwashing to make prophecy comply with what is true and what is false. With all the crap we see on television and hear on radio nowadays, no wonder it seems everybody is going crazy. No one but a few seem to know the truth. No one knows himself or herself today. The reason is that everyone is listening to all those who have the power to make or force you to listen. Now, let's all understand this! There are only a handful of people that will be pulled out of this generation and each of the rest will be left to stand judgment. And those left to stand will watch the world and the word that brought you here in the world, see that very word, and be taken out of the world. Get the message? I do! But no one will be left or taken without first being tried for what you call justice in the American, or the beast, way. Now, none of you has to answer to me at all. I know that for a fact. But, for sure there is one you will answer to. And that very someone is not of your kind or of mine, nor of this world. Or what you may see as your world. I will be there also. To see the greatness of the first and that of the last. I will not be at the far right nor at the far left. But I will be there. For all of my inequities I have explained and forwarded to the most high. And my wait is in the order of prophecy. For none, no not any, can repent on or after that day or time. Because to all those who have lived, that is and was your chance. And all must be done before. Parable: A dead rabbit was to have been aware of the *hunter* with the *gun* coming to kill him before he was shot. Now dead! That very rabbit today—saints. That very rabbit would not be dead today.

Now can anyone out there understand the magic of my gift?

Because I cannot be shaken loose from the tree. Because it is a fruitful tree. Out of a few trees grows the tree of life, for it bears fruit, the fruit of love, faith. If I were you, I would cling to a fig tree. Without doing so, leaves fall, fall off the family tree. Do I now get an amen? But pray and praise the Lord, saints, or are there any saints left out there? Remember what I have said to you, last of a kind, truth of the red blood cell. Let them, and only them, hear what the Spirit says unto the churches. Or are there any left in the church? Because if there are not any people left in the church, then all has been fulfilled. So come! We must hurry. Left are many churches. Their people today are saying to themselves worldwide that the Bible is put too much to the people in bits and pieces, and that the Bible and preacher man do not fully explain to them what it really takes to be saved! But I say this, it's your hearts that are in bits and pieces. Most everyone reads and listens in bits and pieces. Only the things that sound good to each person are taken for self-comfort, self-esteem. If you read in bits, such as the verses that you listen to or the verses that you read to yourselves, then that's the way you will interpret and understand what you read and hear. And this is where the so-called preacher man is. He has led many down the wrong path! Now I say this, I have seen, and know, that the majority of the people today are so confused by this doctrine. I can't blame you for thinking the Bible is false in what is written. But, my brother, it is not! I say this! Those who redo and rewrite, okay. Because it and things will only become worse for them that change the words and for them who believe the words of those who have changed the words.

When you do change that which upsets you, never forget what I have said, and that is: the Bible needs no changing. For it is you that must change. Why is it that it is so hard for so many people to see this? I really don't know? If you will just look at yourselves. You! Yes! You of many faces, weary with problems. You are becoming more and more lost and falling farther away from God. But it's not my words that say this. It was written two thousand years ago. The fools of the earth will

become lost near the end of time. Now, if I can see it and do it
then so can you. But, I repeat, we must all hurry. Man must
either help the preacher man or forget him. I really mean that.
Because we don't have a lifeline or two thousand more years
to change. Maybe you've heard it said many a time before, but
if you have any kind of a brain, see what the world is into now.
Yet you don't believe it, it won't be long. Then what more can I
say to an already lost generation. And why? Is it that so many
so-called preachers are falling and leaving one church and
building another? And what is awful is they are coming up
with so many new names. Now, to my understanding, there were
in the eyes of God only to have been seven churches. Now, do
you know or can you tell me where and why we must have all
these others? If so, you are either very smart or you are very
dumb!

The first and the last, or should I say old, was and is yet
the right. And you, like them of old, have turned your backs
on what was good and for the best. So now for you, and many a
god has done the same. But this time with fear, sorrow, and
much vengeance to all those who have refused to accept the
first and to know and see nowadays why things are like Hell.
Just stop and look! Just who is causing all this hell? I assure
you that it is not God, if you are thinking that. Then think this.

You have joined the rest of the fools in the world! Amen!

Just stop and think and ask yourselves, "Just how smart has
man really become?" Man has fooled only you and himself. Now
do you really not see this? I must say this to all those with little
faith. Have you not noticed that in the last fifty years men's hearts
have grown very, very cold toward one another. It was told
that it would become like such, in Daniel, and St. Matthew's
twenty-fourth chapter. Also in the Book of Revelations, we see
today what is called justice, where a man and the people fight
more for the freedom of the criminal than for that of the victim.
Now just why do you think that is so? The preacher man,
he is so in contempt today, like never before, even though you and
I know it. But you and others don't want to hear it or admit it.
Why? It was written years ago a time would come when, as the
preacher man, he in the very House of the Lord would lead a

many astray. Now do you see this happening today like never before? Truly I say to you all, you know it is very true. The preacher man, his words are not today that of God's word. You may think so! But brothers, it is not! Also, there are those today who have completely given up on trying to believe in God or anyone, no matter what their faith is or was. Religion is becoming a word, to many, of discouragement. And many people today would rather fight you than listen to any more doctrine. Now, in all my studies, 90 percent of all those who have dropped from the churches gave many reasons why. First, because of the swindling preacher man. Second, it was very hard to sit and believe in your neighbor in church. And at the same time, those same saints were seen and known to be doing more wrong than them who were considered on the streets to be misfits! But people, I know the feeling of those that feel that way, and I have also seen it more so day after day. Because many of those out there were forced out onto those very streets. And those who caused them to be put out there won't have a chance of being saved, even though they may think so! At the end, those who think that they have got it made shall be shaken from the very roots of their inequities so that the whole world will see them suffer for what they have done. And many go to church seven days and nights a week. That does not save you! For if in these last days your works are not that of the Living God, when all is being shown to you out in the open, all those things that were said to come will be. And yet you fail to give in? Well! Remember only you can save yourselves. Even if it's the last penny. The churches should not build or spend millions of dollars on construction of such places before feeding all the millions in the world that are starving because ten percent of your gross was not to be for the poor and the rest for your savings accounts. Now, do any of you think that a true God would be among us and give one-third of a group bread and water and give nothing to the rest, who are in the same boat? The churches were set up by God so that they may feed all in need, in the House of the Lord. But do you see this today? No! You do not! But yes! In bits and pieces.

The tidings were the bread and water, to be fed to his people,

not stored and used for your trips around the world, bragging of
what you saw or how many times you've been to the Holy Land.
None of the tidings were meant for you to sanctify yourselves in
splendor. For most of what you had received in the storehouse
was for a very well known purpose. And that purpose is well
known by the preacher man. But again, what do we see him do?
I know! The point is, do you? People! You know very well
God does not need money in Heaven! Everything is and was his
in the first place. And believe you in my teachings. Soon He
will come for what has been loaned to us all! He will claim
everything. For now the time is right. We all know that the
churches have more money, at least ten times more, than our
government. And so, why is it that the governments throughout
the world, and not the church, must try and do so much for the
needy? Because really, it is not their duty to feed God's people.
And truly, all those hypocrites who claim with their tongues to be
from the House of the Lord are not my brothers. I say, wake up
and pray directly to God in these last days, and you will learn
as I have. Directly from him, just what is really going on? Well,
I say what you see is going on is not for the righteous' benefit!
Do I get an amen? I repeat, throughout my writings to you all
with an ear, many, many, times, and that is, history cannot
cannot be changed, especially Bible prophecy. So if you are
looking for comfort and can't find it, remember the very words
of the living God. You will search and search, but won't find
it. Why? Because you, as do many, want everything with the
right hand, and you take at the same time with your left hand
from someone else that which is not yours. So upon this earth,
you have lost both hands.

The order is so that now you cannot receive anything. Do
you now all get the message? Now, to all those that think I
do not speak with the right hand of God's, beware of the beggar
as myself. Look at what is around you. This generation, I truly
say, will find itself very lucky to live past the age of thirty years
old. Just count the young that are being killed in the world
in this decade! It's worse than before in recorded history. And
with all you thought that you knew, yet you still don't know
why? Take my gift.

There is a word *fate,* and there is a word *faith.* Now, which is it that is in your hearts? I will help you recall. For it is fate, not faith. If it was faith, then truly you can and will understand, for what I say to you is not in doctrine. Without it, the world is full of totally confused men just full of anger, violence, and—you see the whole world—just in a mess, with no way out. Pray that you may be able to understand what the Spirit says unto the churches. Again, truly you who are here left standing must hurry! The clock on prophecy is right on time. The angels of the Heavens are at work. The time is right for the harvest. The serpent that had spread the Tares in the fields of the wheat in the land of the valley of God. The wheat is you! Now, my gift is good and true! Beware, for I know my words shall cause hurt and much sadness. But for a few they will bring happiness and some relief. Let it be plainly understood. For do I won't from you! Nor shall I give to you any sorrow in the last day. To the judgment, that will come upon the wicked and the beast!

Remember all I have said to you. And you don't know me! I am from the house of Abraham, David, Solomon, Jacob, Tutankhamen, Moses, and Martin Luther King. I am of the people of Babylon, the son of the father of Ham, who was in the land of Egypt, the brother of the Ethiopian, the second son, the brother of the Sundane's, and the brother of Jordan. I am from what? The House of the LORD!

That of the first and that of the last! My writings are of that! He of the Most High! And for this, my brothers, I cannot, I repeat, I cannot be moved! Even with my powerlessness and the hardness of my words, I cannot end my prophecy to you all. I say this, and that is, there shall be no more prophets to come after the days of Elija. They will come only after the warnings, the sounds of the beggars, the crying of the angels! For they are crying not for You, but because of knowing. Come quickly, because it won't be long.

Ending this book, I say this: Truly you must praise the One God, because he is great!

May God be with you on that day!

9

The News Media–the Tongue

Behold, I am the speaker of the House of the Lord! Now I have this blessing, behold and listen. For I come to you in order to show you the end. That's what is at hand. And there is nothing left within these last hundred years that are not yet fulfilled.

Woe! To you I say woe. For I am the morning and the evening news media; I am the swordsman with the tongue of deceit, better known as the Press. I am given the power to speak out freely—right or wrong. I have the power to topple presidents, or make Presidents, to select a senator, or change a congressman. I am the press, I can overthrow the justice department of any land.

Behold, I, the Press, have caused riots, wars, and upheaval in many lands. I have aided women in their desire to make their law for abortion, for ERA, for adultery, because they want it their way. To them, God is wrong and woman is right. Some people call me the tongue because of my fast maneuvers. I am for the use of anyone that allows me the freedom. I, the News Media—have you not taken the time to notice me?—come into your homes, into your workplaces, and into the subway. I am the Press, the pen, the tongue mightier than the sword!

I, the Media, cause more death than all your guns. I help spread dope and push deceit for your benefit. I lie for you when I print. In many ways, you may say I am the Fork of Satan! And have you not been told of me coming? I am out of the mouth of the dragon. I, the Media, am the strongest of Satan's warriors. In my hand is the pen, my sword, to kill and confuse. I come in favor of all those that are with me to the end. For I, the Media, will break down the very law of the land. And oh, how sweet it is to abound; I am inequity. But you can just call me the Press or Media or whatever turns you on. I, the Press, will pressure the righteous and fulfill the wrongs for your needs in these last days. So hurry, my man, put on your dancing shoes. I'll boogie for you. I am the Press. In order for inequity to abound, I have the right to free speech. I have the right to go and do and say as I please. I, the Press, will make war and death in all the four corners of Hell. Here, I, the tongue, the Media, with the power of Satan, my main man unto me, he hath given me the pen.

I am the news on every street corner in every city, on television, and yet your willingness to stop me is not challenged. I am bold, I open your eyes, your ears, and close your mouth. How great I have become in your Constitution. I am not allowed to speak so freely in my homeland, that of the Great Bear of the far north. So I come forth and use great strength throughout the rest of the world, especially in the land of the free! Here I have the freedom to make believers disbelieve, to change the outcome in a court proceeding. I enter jails, church. I am the free press.

If I, the Press, at any time am refused admission to anything I dislike, I, the Media, shall bring down that very status quo. For I am the backbone, or I am led to believe that I am freedom of speech, not the so-called congressman or mayor. I, the Press, elect or reject all against me. I am the swordsman that was to come for a time. I, the Press, do my job well and no more. Be wise to my tongue. It is death, pain, misery, heartache, misrepresentation, hatred. I bow only to the throne in Hell. And yet, you look the other way in much fear of me and my sword, the pen, in fear that I may speak out against you.

Oh, man of God, what have you in your faith? And where is thy rock you proclaim to stand on? Where is thy mind of righteousness? For while you gather up goodies, diamonds, gold, just as fast as you can, I prepare! So fill your baskets with stupidity and wickedness and I shall take it all away by the scratch of my pen, for I am the Press. I give no thanks to you. I am only your tongue of greed and lust. I only do my job.

But have you so done yours? I am the Media, the Press; you appointed me. You have taken me for my words! I stop and laugh for, because of it, you have given me your life. It belongs to Satan. I was only his warrior. And behold, all this time your God has watched you become a lost fool. And for that you have become me—I—you in the pit of Hell, everlasting with fire and damnation. You had the ear to hear what the Spirit was saying unto the churches, but your tongues and your lust for little faith was like that of many faces.

I, the Press, am great among the weak, the poor, the sly, the warmongers, but don't be upset, for you gave me the power to have free speech. And now I am the pen that's mightier than the sword. So now you weep! I only do my job, and your God has left you. Where can you turn to? Me, the Media! But, I am only you, I am man-made. I am like the four winds. You hear me, and you feel me, but yet you do not see me. Before I take you with me, understand this parable:

Woe, I stop and yell, praise the Lord. Those who live by the sword, shall die by the sword. The sword is your tongue. Your tongue is free to speak of what you dislike and what you fear most and what you sense of the coming of the first Christ, and yet refused to believe in. This is because you are not a god like the one that is and was and is again forevermore.

I, the Press, am you, your ungodliness. I am your disbelief, because you are only you. You deceive you! There is but one God! God is great! Are you? I am the News Media, I am your idol. Believe not in false idols. With my pen, the sword, I print D.E.A.T.H.! Do I get an a-man, for that is all that you are, just a man. I, the Press, am but a dream that can be nothing but that, a dream.

I am the news to your ears, I speak what I want. But I want not of what I speak. For over a thousand years, I have worked for your greed and deceit, and when that day I am no more, then no more shall you be. For you and I, the tongue, you have used it to destroy your very selves.

Woe I say to the gods that are man-made. At the end of time, there shall be not one rock left unturned. Which means all that have tongues to speak shall stand forth to the one almighty God to answer with and for your tongue. And in that day, praise the one God. The very tongue, the mighty sword, the pen, your so-called news media press shall cause you˙ death to the sword. Now do I get an amen? For you have heard of all to come in those last days.

Woe, stop and think, do not talk. But pray with the heart and not the tongue. So now it is time. Praise the Lord! Saints, let your heart and not your tongue be your guide to everlasting life.

A blessing . . . by Brother W. Lee Dawkins.

Pray that you read and understand. Be sure and read all, all of Matthew 14, not one scripture, for your life is at stake.

10

The Prophecy of the Last Days

I will show *everyone,* rich, poor, small, and great, how it was revealed to me through a personal sight of God, and also by many dreams and other dreams to uncover the first dreams. All in order that I may have one purpose, and one purpose only, and that is to show to all—mainly the white race of people—that God is great and that his powers are much greater than Satan's. Also, this book is, to the white race of people, that which was shown to me. They truly do not understand why they are put into the position in the world to rule, as they do today, and for the last two thousand years!

I also am showing how it is that God knows only what you, me, and every human being does. This is whether it be in the daytime or in the night! This is to show every human being you all may think of different things. I'll open up to all how it is that God knows these things before and after!

A man or thing would come and pass through the history of mankind. So remember, I have said many times, that whatsoever it is in a man's heart, then so it is which comes out of his mouth!

Now, let's just all go back to what it was that I said to you at the beginning of my story, of what it really was that I saw at the age of seven. I do know it will be very hard to comprehend something of this magnitude. But even though it is true, I know it will be hard for most people to believe it. Now, let's see if your life is worth trying to save.

Being that I am the one that received the blessings, I offer to those who truly believe in God a chance to accept or reject my offer to them! For my very words shall be proven true. In this generation, from my gifts, many people of the whole world shall hear and gain knowledge. Also wisdom, this wisdom that is of a man, who is and is not of this world! The most important thing in this is to show you the true powers of God.

Remember, God himself stated in the last Book of Revelations, that in the very last days before his coming, that He—God—would pour out to some people a gift that would startle the world in what they would show many unbelievers. It would shake the world. How could it be that a mere man, as myself and others, are to do certain things of an unbelievable nature, such as what I have written and will write to you. This I was shown shall shake the souls of many, of millions.

Throughout the whole world, those who read understand what I write. Now, to *each* individual, a gift or gifts may come to an individual in different ways! As for mine, it has been shown through many dreams, but the best was through the onset of the real thing at the age of seven. Through each dream, each dream has come true, as in so many days allowed for each, only when the time was shown to be right. God is aware of each individual's thoughts and works, plus what is in their hearts.

Now here is knowledge! Take this parable of what it was that I saw:

There stood a man in broad daylight, standing in the mist of Heaven! He was standing there among all of the stars in the Heaven. As I looked at the face of the man who stood in the mist he had a head which was made out of the blending of a few stars. I could not describe the features of the man's face nor his color. Yet it was of a man. He was clothed in white, as a robe. The robe was as white as snow! And the collar had the shape of a V. The lining around the neck was made of pure gold. Also, another lining was about his feet, which also had a lining with the same description as the top lining. It too was lined with pure gold. It was of the purest of all golds. And the white robe was the purest of all white silky linings. Now, each one of his hands were made from a cluster of stars. I was allowed to see this much of the man who stood in the mist of the Heaven and within the mist of the stars in all of the universe.

Now, understand you this next sight, because if you can,

then you can understand how it is that God knows exactly what we all think and do in our everyday lives! Again, as I looked at the man clothed in white, he comforted me in time of danger and spoke to me. I could then see that he was inside of all of the Heavens, and yet . . . the entire Heavens were inside of him! Then it was again that the man, clothed in pure white linen, was outside of all the Heavens and the earth. The earth was in his very hand reach. But even though earth to me was so far away from his hand, as I stood looking at him, I felt then by what he told and showed me that, to him, the earth was so near, as if it were already in the palm of his mighty hands.

I won't imagine, because I know, but imagine our very own blood cells. For we all know that blood travels throughout all our bodies. So does air! These two also must go through the brain of every living thing! Both the air for oxygen and blood for the feeding and nourishment of the soul and for life. In other words, then, the brain knows everything about its individual body. Right? So as the blood and air travels throughout the brain, the brain then analyzes each blood cell, checking on each cell individually! This is for its purity. It also has white blood cells. These white cells are supposed to protect the red cells from any and all matter—so we learn! Right? That is, they protect from all outside matter, like air, but not the blood. The air comes and it goes from the body—right or wrong? You, now, must remember that God is the Spirit, as the wind. Right? That which is of the air, that which we must all breathe to live and survive.

Now, here is the wisdom of what I saw and learned from the man clothed in white: The man clothed in white was inside of us all, as is the blood and the air. We were inside of the man, who was clothed in white. Just as the stars were within him. The man in the Heavens. Yet he was also out of the Heavens. He had to have such power as I have, to do such a thing. Also, the man in white could do the same too, being of free spirit and of the air. Also, being of every living cell which was of the air and the blood. This I was shown with these powers. The Almighty God could travel in and out of us and every living thing so long as we all must have air and water! That meant that no living thing could live without, first and always, going through the brain of the man I saw standing in the mist among all of the stars. Now, can a wise man uncover the might of the one God?

Now, this was my most blessed of all of the blessings, that I alone had received. For this I claim there are no, I repeat, there are no gods but the one God! For Ala ist! Ak'ba! Praise the Lord! The speech and my writings are for everyone who has an ear. Let it be that each understands what it is that the spirits are saying to the people and the churches. Most of all to the crooked preacher men! They who have failed to teach the true words of God!

Behold the preachers of men. The people have come and they have knocked at your doors, but yet you have led them astray, damning the truthful at heart. You, the preachers of men, have damned yourselves, all of those who fail to accept. Then truly time won't belong. To belong. I had this dream. That again this generation that you now see shall not pass.

Take a final parable as my gift!

If a wise man, say, filled up his car's gas tank to travel thirty to forty miles to get to his place of destination, then he would more than likely not worry about getting there, borrowing no other problems, right? Then, so shall it be, I was shown that it is the same for travelers who are on the way to heaven! There is one gas station, with only one fill-up. Only one stop allowed to be made for gas. The long road is narrow and crooked. But, with the right amount of gas and a full tank, it is possible for you as a traveler to get there in front of the gates. But to enter, you all must come prepared.

Amen. Now, here is my own personal speech to and for the master race, better known as the white race, and it is: This book was written mainly to you, not because you are hated by me, but because I was shown that the white race was shown to be the same as the title of this book! Also, there are those of the white race who do understand and have a chance to be saved, if once they see and learn the truth. That is why things are as they seem, and are the ways and meaning of your race. This is also to the many who have joined you in doing your ways, the ways of the whites, even though they are not white, but are seen as whites in the eyes of God. Because they, too, did, and are doing, the ways of the whites. Now, if there was no love in my heart for such a race, like the whites, then I would not have written this book! For it is only written in order to show the whites the true way, now, so they can be men as are other men, whether they be black, yellow, red, or blue! You, the white, should not hate me for my gift. But be you a bit thankful for what I have been allowed to show you is what you may think is right, even though your ways are wrong. Because, most important, I would lay down my life for you, the whites, and I have many times. Also, you were to me as a close friend, because I really would like to see all of us get to Jesus. Or as many as I thought who cared or wanted to go.

So remember, is it just that one man, because of his color, cannot show power? Or make good speeches, or have the money to build and destroy? This does not mean that others are not given even greater powers than yours, powers that show the wonders of God!

As for myself, I am a beggar. Also, if I didn't care about helping you to go where I pray to go, then it would not be in my heart to try and show you anything! For the blessing is mine and only mine, given only to me! But I stopped, I paused to share my gifts with you, all the whites of the world. I say, fear not the color of a man's skin, but fear God, because he and he alone is the one that, whether right or whether wrong, you all must face at the stroke of time! It won't be long . . . to belong. My book is for wisdom!

It is for the taking, like that old song goes: "Just reach out and touch somebody's hand. And we would all make this world a better place if we did."

To love and know you as my brother, which I am, even though you have denied me because of my color. Then shall you also deny me a chance to show you! To save you?

Amen.

11

The Message to the Moral Majority

Now to finalize my point to the Moral Majority. Let me show them what I've been shown. Take heed that you understand. For your tongues may it seem wise, and may your hearts be weak, for all the tidings that you have received and yet still do receive from all those that have little faith! But, I say to all those, that the day shall come that what all you have taken and misused for self must, I repeat, must, be repaid in full. For it is said by God Almighty of what you preach: That what you sow is what you reap! Then also remember, so shall your thoughts and works be unto you, the preacher men.

Truly I say unto you all, the preachers of man, the days of yours are limited. For did not God himself show anger and destroy the synagogues in the days of old, two thousand years ago? Let me clue you all for the very same reason as we see it more and more today in and around most churches. For it is that the house of the Lord has become very unfavorable to what is going on in the churches of today and to their real goals. This is without doubt! For what is the true image of God? Truly it is not that of greed, nor is it to *beg* each day, or to proclaim great blessings which are not that of the true God, but the old familiar thing, the dollar bill.

I know your ways, and yet I am but a beggar. Praise the Lord! Then how shall it be said of you, the Moral Majority? Take a Parable:

For when a lion's belly is full after a kill for food, then does he kill again before the next meal is due? No! Nor does he kill to have extra food around for a later day. For the lion, knowing very well that the next day may never come, only lives

for that one day. Because, even for him, the lion, his days are
limited. Besides, not even a snake would do such.

But, I say this, can it be? O preacher man, those of the
Moral Majority, you preach and gather all of the monies to
live! Or is it that you live to gather all of the money? For yet I
know! I say again, for there are none, I repeat, *none* greater
than God and his ways of the world. You must truly realize this.
For your works, I have a dream to the righteous of the preacher
man. May he alone understand that you are not yet born again
until the last coming of Christ to judge you and also myself. But
would it not be funny to see you, the preacher man, left standing
when comes the day of rapture? Amen.

Now here is the guide I was shown to uncover to all how to
find the *Beast of Revelation* of Chapter 13:

Now to unlock to you the dragon and the beast. You must be
sure, as I have stated before, you all must be sure and read all the
chapters from beginning to end. Also, each chapter must be read
in the exact order I have them. And, the second most important
thing, always stop and think after each chapter, and give much
thought to the chapter you have just completed before going on
to the next chapter. The third most important thing is, be wise
and put together what race of people fits the description of the
dragon or the beast, which are spoken of in and throughout the
chapters, and flow to and from the beginning unto the end of
time as was foreseen. I have had a dream, and that dream, I say,
won't be long! To belong! So praise the one God! That each
and all do without doubt! Pray that you understand just what
it is the spirits are saying unto the churches!

Look back into history, as far back as two thousand years
or more; after this book, there is no more to come. For once
you have unlocked the mystery of the beast and the dragon,
and know the race and the color of it, then you should have
peace of mind at last, and be able to give each and every human
being the reason why things are as they are in this world.
Again, make it known to everyone, make no mistakes, because
I say at last to all that have an ear—that is Bible prophecy!
It is right on time according to Jesus Christ. Only will a wise

man or woman understand the man with the number; I say, six three times three and six!

I have promised you the man with the number 6/?/6.

Let a wise man understand the number six three times three and six! For here is wisdom. The seventeen industrial nations are all of the dragon, which is Magog, which is of the Antichrist, which is of the free world. Which are the ten horns plus *two?* Old Germany and the Japanese Empire; now both have fallen. Add six. That equals twenty-three. Twenty-three minus five equals eighteen. Now of the new ten plus two equals twelve. These are all of the dragon, or the so-called free world.

Again be wise of the parting of the man, who is of the beast! For now comes twenty-one minus twelve equals nine, which is that of Russia and its allies: Poland, Hungary, Ethiopia, Lybia, Syria, Romania, Czechoslovakia, and Persia. These are of Gog, also known as the beast spoken of in Revelations, Chapter 13. Now, six plus nine equals fifteen, the number of a man! Is six three times three, which is nine threescore, then there comes the six. The two left out of twenty-three are no more, Rome and that of Alexander the Great.

Praise the Lord! Saints that you understand for what it is that the Spirit says unto the churches.

The beast and the dragon and the race of the beast

1.	Magog	1.	The slain beast
2.	Antichrist	2.	Gog
3.	America	3.	Russia

READ: Guide to uncover the beast and the Four Horsemen.

1. Revelation, chapters 13 and 14.
2. Revelation, chapter 9, entirely.
3. Peter, chapter 3.
4. Timothy, chapter 3.

5. St. Matthew, chapters 23 and 24.
6. St. Matthew, chapter 15, entirely—very important.
7. St. Matthew, chapter 13, entirely—very important.
8. St. Matthew, chapter 10, entirely!
9. Malachi, chapter 3—very important for the preacher man.
10. Daniel, chapter 2—America and Russia as of today.
11. Daniel, chapter 12—very important, about number of years!
12. Daniel, chapter 2, entirely from verse 1 through verse 49.
13. Ezekiel, chapter 38—of America and Russia.
14. Jeremiah, chapter 19—history of America and Russia and Europe.
15. Isaiah, chapters 55, 56—of America and the black man.
16. Genesis, chapter 10—the true Jew, the sons of Ham and Lands.
17. Genesis, chapter 2—where the Garden of Eden is, no doubt!
18. Numbers, Chapters 1 through 16: What skin color (white) meant in God's eyes.

All of these chapters will without a doubt show the entire world why things are as they are in this world. The most important thing it does is show who is the master race and why! Where do they live, what is their color. They show the mark of the beast and just who is the Antichrist spoken of to come. They also show who Gog is. Also, who is Magog? Truly, the answers are within your own hearts.

12

Could Dictator or Antichrist Begin?

Now to awake those that truly believe in God! Let me show you all the last signs and warnings. Pray that you understand. And for that I say this. If you are very wise, to see the works of the so-called Moral Majority. For it is in prophecy of them. If not aware of what you may think is true, or what might you think is false. For in those last days, there shall arise a dictatorship. Not by me but by their very own tongues. The Holy Scripture speaks of this to come near the end of time. Now, here is my gift to those who have an ear. A gift given to me from the Most High! For yet we see the Moral Majority stating worldwide, more so out of America, that if all those in and out of government fail to go along with what they want, President Ronald Reagan and all his followers must be done. Then they, the Moral Majority, will do all that they can. To see to it, their power will try to topple that very status quo? But I say be not afraid, but be wise so that you may truly understand. For what I say unto the churches, this may just be the beginning of the Antichrist, and the beginning of a so-called dictatorship. For yet a many may not want to see or hear of what I say unto you. But will you make me a wager? In a not so very long time you will see as I have been shown, that all I say unto you, the true Believers. Remember, beware of the beggar. For I am the last of a kind. For those with an ear, let them only hear what is being said unto the church of God. And be most aware of those that promise you Glory before the time has come. For only your hearts, which are of your Brain, hold the might of faith! And never forget, that glory will come to you, because you can not go to glory. For God himself had stated, that upon his return, He would come with great glory. And that glory would be given to all those who did not have the mark of the beast in their hand or upon their foreheads. Now, here is another gift just to show you the power of my mind that has been given unto me? Now you figure this out! Of the number six threescore and six, is it to you that the number threescore does total six? Or could the number which is in threescore be that of nine? For yet I know! Now the gift is of this. Some will think and say *"Six, six, and six."* And again I say six, nine, and six. Why? But first let me aid you a little bit. For only the righteous shall understand. If prophecy was meant to show everyone so easy, the man with the number six threescore and six, then why was it put not as six, six, and six? Be it to you wise, for all is a work of God! To put mathematics in such a form was only to confuse the Wicked.

For God himself said, let a wise man unlock that number of a man. Now I say this to you all. If it was meant for it to be that easy, to figure out that number, then it would not have been put forth in such a manner. Now do I get an amen? Praise the Lord! Saints? Here now is a parable to the righteous of the world. From my gift! If each day you saw the sun rise from the east, you would know then that it was the break of day. And in that same day you saw the Sun set in the west, you then would know that it was the end of that day. Right? And no weatherman would have to tell you day after day just what time the sun would come up and what time it would go down. Right? For with *your own eyes* you would know. Then so shall it be in this generation, that you and all shall see total prophecy— *the rise and the fall* which is that of the end of prophecy. Because Jesus has laid it all right before each and everyone's eyes. Now I ask this, would you give a begger a dime for his asking? Or would you give him a dime for his needs? Praise the Lord that you understand of what it was that the beggar was asking you for? For the same is what you ask of God! Which is like that of a beggar. For it is not really for a dime. But beware of the tramp. Because the meek are wiser than they with all the gold, silver, and money in the storehouse. The meek are like that of a camel about to enter the eye of the needle. And to those with greed and no hunger, the weight of lust shall hold you from ever entering the streets of gold that lie beyond the eye of that needle. Now, do I get an amen? I say this, brothers and sisters, God has confused the dragon and the beast so much so that they of the children of the whore of Revelation 13 and 14 cannot be awakened to my gift. For I know that they will surely be fearsome, and shall go out even more so to slay and kill! And by this, do you think this is love for God? Just because things all of a sudden are not going their way? For now their powers are that of Satan. And for sure it spells self-destruction. And what is really good about it all is that God knew it before the beginning of time. He knew the final outcome. Praise the LORD. Now just what people do you think will sing "Hal-le-luja" at the very end? For sure a fool won't! For sure a rich man won't. For sure a dictator won't! For sure the beast won't. For sure the Antichrist won't. And for very, very sure Satan won't! Now praise the Lord. Because I am of the beggar. And also I have been shown why it was that Elija would be the last prophet of God. And the very reason was this, because of the beast and all those that did and would become part of the beast, as we all see it and him today. For the teachers of most, I state most churches have used the house of the Lord as that of a business and not that of a preacher or of a prophet. For in those days of our Lord Jesus and his twelve disciples, when they did go out not once did they ask for bread or use their blessing as a business. Because even then, some of them had businesses but gave them up! They knew that with that man called Jesus they would have more than money in the storehouse, knowing very well that they couldn't take it with them.

While sitting here in a pause, I had my television on. And I stop to watch Canadian Channel Two on cable. And there sits this woman speaking in wonders. Now, this is being seen nationwide, I am sure. She stated that the Holy Spirit was a female. She goes on to say that while she was reading a few verses in the Bible, that she noted that God said let us make man and woman in our own image. And that God was at that time speaking to a female! But praise the Lord that you understand. Be not the fool. For I say this as God had created man as a living soul. At that time and even before, God created angels for them to look over and confirm all of his wonders, and that was whom he spoke unto! Because the angels were that of the spirits, nothing more. Now to clarify my statement. See! For in the beginning was the beginning and the beginning was the Word and the Word was God! Not gods and the female god. For I show myself to all who are being misled. Come quickly, for we must truly hurry. I am the beggar at your doorstep. And yet, your hearts will not open. Remember! There shall be a many that will come in His name and show great wonders, but not me! Because I am like a grain of sand that was put into form just to be a beggar or a tramp. But most of all, pray that you understand. Because I show you that time as we once knew it! It shows to be very short, so short that the tears from your eyes may not ever have time to reach the ground. Also, let a wise man, in all the world, show me or you a white man that will bow down and let himself be judged by another race of people? Pray that you understand my words. Those of a beggar! Now, again show me a race of people that does not bow down to the white race for all their needs and wants! And show me a people or a land today that would dare go up against the beast of the north with the feet of a bear. And the dragon of the north? For they, that people of all the northern parts, shall rule until the end of time. And I say verily, it is bible prophecy. And no person on earth can change prophecy. And in these last days, the dragon and the beast have become so bold and so strong, no one can stand up against him. And for any man or woman or child that can understand and change out of the white race, be wise enough to pray for what is right and live in accord. Then you have been saved! And I repeat, show me another man that will fit the description, other than that of the master race, and I will show you the universe in the palm of your hand.

So count the number six threescore and six. At the same time, pray that you are not a complete fool! For I am in total shock to see America, the greatest that ever was in the whole world, be so stupid as to continue feeding the great bear of the north. And also feeding Persia. For what America has done is this. It has put a rope around the necks of God's chosen people, the Israelis. Even though yet, you, America, do not see it that way. Your aid is but only aid to prophecy to overrun Israel.

Message to the Jews of God and his beloved Jews. I understand your pain now in Israel but fear not, for all my forefather's prayers shall come to your light at this generation's end. Then, and only then, shall you believe that your God and mine is real. But not until then shall you believe.